The
CONGRESS

The CONGRESS

by Leslie Gourse

★ ★ ★

Franklin Watts
New York / Chicago / London / Toronto / Sydney
A First Book

Cover photograph copyright © Jay Mallin

Photographs copyright ©: Jay Mallin: pp. 6, 8 bottom, 11, 59 bottom; Library of Congress: pp. 8 top, 16, 17; Bettmann Archive: pp. 8 center, 9 top right, 18, 45; Wide World Photos: pp. 9 top left, 28, 31, 57, 58; Washington Convention and Visitors Association: p. 9 bottom; North Wind Picture Archives: pp. 10, 20, 22; Virginia State Library and Archives: p. 15; UPI/Bettmann: pp. 34, 35; Reuters/ Bettmann: pp. 42, 43; Gamma-Liaison/Brad Markel: pp. 48, 59 top; Lyndon Baines Johnson Library/*Austin Statesman*: p. 50; Archive Photos/Arnold Sachs: p. 51

Library of Congress Cataloging-in-Publication Data

Gourse, Leslie.
    The congress / Leslie Gourse.
    p. cm. — (A First book)
    Includes bibliographical references and index.
      ISBN 0-531-20178-3
      1. United States. Congress — Juvenile literature. [1. United States — Congress.]
    I. Title. II. Series.
    JK1061.G66 1994
    328.73'07 — dc20   94-962
                         CIP AC

MAY '96

Contents

Chapter 1

Congress Today

Congress, the lawmaking branch of the United States government, meets in the Capitol, a huge white building with a cast-iron dome in Washington, D.C. On top of the dome perches a $19\frac{1}{2}$-foot-high (5.9-m) statue of Freedom. Contractors and workmen used nearly nine million tons of cast iron to build the dome. That gives you an idea of the enormous size and majesty of the building and of the architects' estimation of the importance of Congress. The building sits on top of Capitol Hill, originally called Jenkins's Hill.

George Washington was president when funds were first allocated to start building the Capitol. The first architects were inspired by the design of the great buildings and temples of ancient Greece. Only a portion of the Capitol, made of sandstone from Virginia, was finished when Congress moved into it in 1780.

Washington, D.C., was then a small settlement on the Potomac River. When Congress was formed, nobody had any idea how powerful and complicated it would become as the country grew bigger and more populous. More states

In 1814, the Capitol (top) burned and was rebuilt. By 1851, the building had taken on a familiar form and Washington, D.C., was growing quickly (middle). (Left) A close-up of Armed Freedom.

(Top) *Armed Freedom,* the statue that tops the
Capitol dome, was removed for cleaning in
1993. (Middle) In 1863, in the midst of the
Civil War, construction continued to expand
the Capitol building. (Left) Today, the Capitol
and its surroundings have very little resem-
blance to the city as it was in 1851.

The Library of Congress was begun as a source of information for members of Congress. The initial collection was from Thomas Jefferson's library and soon outgrew its space. The Library's chief responsibility is still to the Congress members.

entered the Union, and more senators and representatives—the lawmakers who serve elected terms in Congress—went to work in Washington.

As time went by, congressmen needed so much more office space that six new buildings were constructed to house them and their staffs. Representatives now have offices in three buildings on the south side of the Capitol, along Independence Avenue. The buildings are named in honor of three illustrious Speakers of the House of Representatives: Cannon, Longworth, and Rayburn. Senators' offices are located in the Russell, Dirksen, and Hart buildings. Named in honor of Senate majority leaders, the Senate buildings stand on the north side of the Capitol, on Constitution Avenue. Until the first office buildings opened, representatives and senators worked at their cluttered desks in the legislative chambers, right where they sat to vote on proposed laws.

When the Capitol was made bigger and more modern, and the amount of business became more time-consuming, a

A special subway links the congressional office buildings to Capitol Hill. It can only be used by members of Congress and their staffs.

system of buzzers and lights was installed to summon representatives and senators to their chambers to vote.

This great complex of buildings is a far cry from the simple beginnings of Congress, when there were only thirteen states sending representatives and senators to serve as the nation's legislators. Now there are one hundred senators, two from each of the fifty states. The House of Representatives has 435 members, with the most populous states sending the most representatives. Each one represents a congressional district in a state. However, when Alaska and Hawaii became states in the middle of this century, each was allowed to send only one person to the House of Representatives, because it was feared that Congress would become too big and unwieldy. Hawaii now has two representatives, while Alaska still has only one. There are also delegates from Washington, which is the District of Columbia, American Samoa, Guam, and the Virgin Islands as well as a resident commissioner from the Commonwealth of Puerto Rico.

Let's clear up one point that could lead to confusion later on. Members of the House of Representatives are sometimes called congressmen and congresswomen, and sometimes they're called representatives. Senators are usually not referred to as congressmen or congresswomen; they're traditionally called senators. But technically a senator is also a congress-

man or congresswoman—that is, a member of Congress—
just as a representative is.

The basic law of the United States, a document called the
Constitution, requires that Congress meet, or assemble, every
year, on January 3, at noon. Congressmen and congresswomen can appoint another day, if they need to.

Chapter 2

The Founding of Congress

The Constitution of the United States, which provided for the creation of Congress and other branches of the government, was written by pioneers in a new land. They were accustomed to being independent in spirit and thought. The way they came to write their visionary ideas into the Constitution puts the work of Congress into perspective.

The thirteen colonies of America began a full-fledged revolution against the king of England in 1775. The Revolutionary War started in Massachusetts with "the shot heard round the world." The colonies hadn't formed a real country then. They didn't have a president or a Supreme Court or a Congress to enact their own laws. All the colonies had was a common desire to free themselves from British rule.

In 1776, bright young patriots from the colonies—among them businessmen, lawyers, doctors, teachers, and farmers—met in Philadelphia. Their group was called the Continental Congress. Among these patriots were George Washington from the colony of Virginia and John Adams from

Massachusetts. Patrick Henry and Thomas Jefferson came from Virginia too, both of them young and well educated. Jefferson, a talented writer and speaker, was a planter and had just built his own house, called Monticello, but he was fascinated by the political struggle of the colonists. Men also came from the colonies of New York, New Jersey, Rhode Island, North Carolina, South Carolina, Georgia, Maryland, Connecticut, Delaware, Pennsylvania, and New Hampshire.

The colonists had never had a voice in the British government, so Jefferson—a tall, freckle-faced, red-haired man—was asked to write a document that would announce the independence of America. The men called this document the Declaration of Independence. It says that people sometimes need to declare their independence and form a new country in which citizens will have the God-given right to "life, liberty and the pursuit of happiness." Those words would become

General George Washington led American troops to victory and was elected the first president of the United States.

John Adams (right) and
Thomas Jefferson (below)

among the most famous in the Declaration of Independence.

At the end of the Declaration, Jefferson and the other writers said the patriots at the meeting were acting as representatives of the United States of America to declare the independence of the colonies from the British Crown. As an independent country, the United States of America had full power to declare war, agree to peace, enter into alliances and make agreements with other countries, and take any actions that free and independent states had the right to do. The Declaration of Independence ends with these words: "And for the support of this Declaration, with a firm reliance on the

protection of Divine Providence, we mutually pledge to each other our lives, our fortunes and our sacred honor."

Dressed in knee breeches and ruffled silk shirts, the representatives to the Continental Congress dipped their quill pens in ink and signed their names to the Declaration of Independence and adopted it on July 4, 1776. They knew that the British could hang them for signing that document, but they put their lives on the line for their passionate desire for independence.

They elected George Washington to be commander in chief and to lead the Continental Army. The Revolutionary

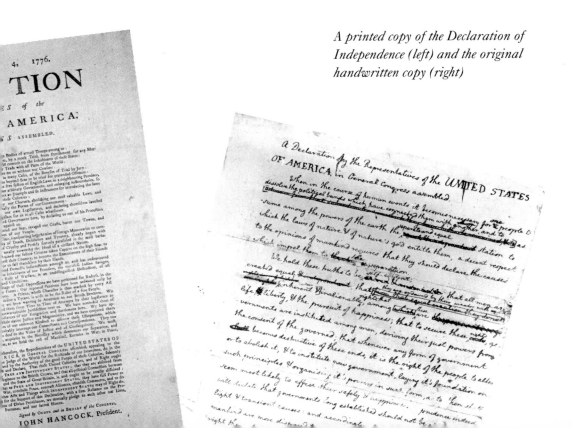

A printed copy of the Declaration of Independence (left) and the original handwritten copy (right)

John Adams proposes George Washington as the commander in chief of the Continental Army.

War was long and bitterly fought. The Americans won in 1781, five years after the colonists had signed the Declaration of Independence. That was the year all the fighting ended. The formal peace treaty was signed in 1783. Then the country governed itself under the Articles of Confederation written by the Constitutional Convention. George Washington went home to his plantation, Mount Vernon, thinking he could finally live a quiet life.

But the citizens of the confederation of thirteen separate states discovered that their alliance couldn't survive without a truly unifying government. The states were fighting with each other. For one thing, they didn't have a unifying money system. One state's money couldn't be spent in another state. A man from New Jersey couldn't sell his goods in New York because the money offered to him in New York was useless in New Jersey. That was one of many problems threatening to destroy the confederation of states.

So some of the signers of the Declaration of Independence decided to return to Philadelphia in 1789 for a new Constitutional Convention. They closed the shutters of their meeting room because they didn't want anybody to eavesdrop on what they were saying. There were so many different opinions among people outside the room about what the laws of the country should be that people might start to fight. Even the men inside the room argued about what rights the new central government should have. Rhode Island was so opposed to the purpose of the meeting that the state didn't send a representative.

Some men, like John Adams of Massachusetts, thought a democratic republic with equal representation for all people was a bad idea; he didn't believe that people could rule themselves. People who agreed with him were called Federalists. Many of them were bankers and businessmen from the Northeast. Others, who agreed with Thomas Jefferson's idea that all men were created equal, were called Republicans or Democratic Republicans.

The needs of the agricultural South (above) and those of the industrial North (below) brought about compromises that shaped the final form of the U.S. Constitution and federal government.

Generally speaking, the Southerners at the meeting represented the interests of farmers and planters. The Northerners represented the commercial interests predominant in their states. Each representative wanted to preserve his own state's interests in the union. Some men wanted a strong central government. And some wanted the state governments to have all the power.

The men compromised on many details and emerged from the meeting with a remarkable document—the Constitution. Among the amazing things it provided for was a government with three branches—a president as head of the executive branch for administration of the country; a Supreme Court as the top court in the nation's legal system, known as the judicial branch; and the Congress as the law-making body, known as the legislative branch. The men elected George Washington, a Republican, to serve as the first President of the United States. John Adams, a Federalist, became the first Vice President.

Later, ten amendments were added to the Constitution to ensure the individual freedom and rights of all citizens of the United States. These first ten amendments became known as the Bill of Rights. They were ratified, or approved, by three-quarters of the states.

The Bill of Rights guaranteed every man freedom of religion, freedom of speech, and freedom of the press. It granted

The Bill of Rights, the first ten amendments to the U.S. Constitution, guaranteed important freedoms, including freedom of the press.

freedom to assemble, too. That meant that people could meet to discuss whatever they wanted, as long as they didn't plot the illegal or violent overthrow of the government. The Bill of Rights also guaranteed freedom from tyranny by the militia—the armed forces—and from illegal search and seizure, and it provided that people accused of crimes should be protected from "cruel and unusual punishments."

Not everybody who wrote the Constitution and its Bill of Rights approved of freedom of religion. And it took a long time to truly enforce freedom of the press. Newspaper publishers occasionally went to jail if they opposed the president's policies. It also took a very long time—and a cruel and bloody Civil War—for the country to outlaw slavery. Slaves had none of the freedoms guaranteed by the Constitution and the Bill of Rights. But the seeds of freedom were planted in the Constitution and the Bill of Rights.

It was the duty of Congress to make laws for all Americans, based on the provisions in the Constitution and the Bill of Rights. Through the years, Congress has written thousands of laws to deal with the growing and changing country. The basic principles, as set down by the founders, for those laws have not changed to this day.

Chapter 3

How Congress Works

Because of their differing political beliefs, the founders of the country formed two political parties: the Federalists, who believed in a strong central government, and the Democratic Republicans, who wanted the states to hold most of the power. The tug-of-war between these two parties helped to establish a balance in the new country by fostering debate and tolerance for the opinions of others. The tradition of political parties in the United States began with these two groups.

Most senators and representatives in the twentieth century have been either Democrats or Republicans. The United States government has nearly always run on a two-party system. One side or the other needs a clear majority, more than 50 percent of the votes, to win an election. There's no legal limit to the number of parties the country can have. And the Constitution does not require the country to have any political parties at all. But the founders wanted a government in which the majority ruled, and it is more difficult for a candidate to win a majority of the votes if more than two people are running for office. Once candidates for office have won seats in the Senate or the House of Representatives, usually either as Democrats or Republicans, they continue to maintain strong ties with their party.

Making the Nation's Laws

As we have said, the primary job of Congress is to write the nation's laws, and to change and amend existing laws. Ideas for laws begin in several ways. Sometimes candidates for office are elected because they have promised to help pass certain laws. Or a member of Congress may become aware of the need for a new law and introduce the idea. Or a special interest group may petition a member of Congress to get a law passed. The president can send Congress his ideas and requests for laws, too. And there are executive communications, which are letters from the executive branch—that is, from the president or a member of his cabinet or an independent agency—suggesting new laws to Congress. But according to the Constitution, it is Congress that has final responsibiity for introducing and shaping ideas of all kinds and passing them into laws.

The Senate and the House of Representatives cooperate in making most laws, but sometimes the Senate alone or the House alone will pass a bill that affects only itself. Both houses have the right to introduce bills of most kinds, but only the House of Representatives can initiate revenue bills, which have to do with money. This provision gives the House of Representatives a very great power, known as "the power of the purse." It's up to the House of Representatives to allocate funds and vote for the financing of all government programs. Most legislation on all kinds of matters starts in the House of Representatives. After one house writes a bill and votes to pass it, that house sends it to the other house of Congress for its approval.

The President's Veto Power

A law is called a bill until it is approved and becomes a law. Most often, a bill needs the approval of the president after both houses have voted yea. To keep alive the early spirit of the country, congressmen use the old-fashioned traditional words "yea" and "nay" when they vote. A bill can become law without the president's approval if he doesn't send the bill back to Congress with his objections within ten days of receiving it. If Congress adjourns before those ten days elapse, the bill withheld or disapproved by the president doesn't become law. But even if the president vetoes, or refuses to sign a bill approved by Congress, that bill can still be passed into law if Congress can raise enough votes—a two-thirds majority in both houses—to override a president's veto. These provisions are part of the system of checks and balances provided in the Constitution to ensure that no one branch of the government acquires too much power over the other branches.

Getting Elected to Congress

Two senators are elected from each state for a term of six years each. Every two years the country has an election to replace or reelect one-third of the senators—those who have completed their six-year terms in office. The whole Senate is never replaced or reelected at one time. The senator who has been in office for the longest time is called the senior senator from his or her state, while the other one is known as the junior senator.

To run for election and serve in the Senate, a man or woman must be thirty years old at the start of a term. All senators must live in the states they represent. Senators can be born in foreign countries, but they have to be citizens of the United States for nine years before they are permitted to run for the Senate.

Elections for the 435 seats in the House of Representatives take place every two years. Candidates for the House of Representatives must be twenty-five years of age. They must live in the states they represent. And they must be U.S. citizens for at least seven years before starting their terms of office.

To become members of Congress, candidates must first run an election campaign. After being elected to Congress,

Dianne Feinstein campaigns for the U.S. Senate. Californians elected her and Barbara Boxer to the Senate in 1992. This was the first time in U.S. history that both senators from a state were women.

they must take care of the business of writing the nation's laws and overseeing the operation of the federal government. At the same time, members of Congress—both senators and representatives—must stay in touch with the people who elected them. Election campaigns never really end for members of Congress who want to do their jobs correctly and serve repeated terms. So representatives and senators stay very busy keeping in touch with voters—finding out what they want and telling them what is going on—and carrying on the work of Congress.

Keeping in Touch with the Voters

Legislators use several important tools to reach the voters. The most powerful of these tools is television. Since the 1950s, televised hearings in the Senate and House of Representatives have become very popular. When bills are very important, sensitive, or controversial, committees in charge of the bill schedule public hearings. Hearings by committees are required by law to be open to the public except when a majority of people on a committee decide that open hearings could endanger national security or violate a rule of the house. Televised hearings can make celebrities out of members of Congress. Their faces become familiar to people across the country. And this fame can be important in their getting reelected. Televised or not, hearings on sensitive issues can give legislators a chance to get their names in the news.

All representatives and senators need television exposure to bolster their reputations. If they don't get a chance to appear in televised congressional hearings, they sometimes send tapes of themselves, called video feeds, to their local television stations. The films keep the voters informed about the activities of their elected officials in Washington. Some members of Congress want to gain popularity so they can become important, conscientious leaders. Other members of Congress simply want to become celebrities. Nearly all of them want to be reelected.

Historically, Congress—the Senate more so than the House—has always resembled an exclusive club. The six-year terms of office for senators allow them time to form friendships with influential members and to establish a position of importance in the Senate. Before the advent of television, members of Congress depended primarily upon these relationships with each other to build their popularity and to give them a chance to serve on various committees. But television has changed this tradition. Now senators and representatives depend on TV appearances to make them popular and to build up their esteem.

Video tapes are expensive to produce. In the Senate, they are paid for by the taxpayers. The House of Representatives does not allow its members to use public funds to make video tapes. But both senators and representatives can use the TV studios in the Capitol free of charge.

Members of Congress can also send out letters, free of charge, thanks to a privilege known as franking. A frank is a

Senate and House leaders have found television a valuable tool in communicating their opinions to their constituents back home.

copy of a legislator's signature on an envelope in place of a postage stamp. This privilege allows legislators to send out enormous quantities of mail to voters without having to pay for stamps. Today's legislators send vast amounts of campaign mail churned out by copying machines, computers, printers, automated letter folders, and mass mailing systems. The cost of congressional mailings rose to more than $100 million in the mid–1980s.

Another important tool that members of Congress use to keep in touch with the folks back home is known as casework. Voters can write to their representative and ask for help or information. A question can be about Social Security, health care, insurance, military service, loans for education and small businesses, or anything at all. Congressional staff members respond to these letters and do favors for voters. Members of Congress endear themselves to voters by providing this kind of personal attention.

Representatives and senators also make trips back home to appear in person before voters. Elected officials must constantly raise funds from voters to pay for their next election campaigns. Legislators sometimes use funds raised from supporters to pay for public opinion polls. Through direct, personal questions in polls, legislators find out what the voters are thinking about and what they want to see done.

So television, franking, casework, personal appearances,

and opinion polls are five of the most important tools and perks, or perquisites—privileges—that members of Congress use to stay in touch with voters and to prepare for reelection. At the same time, legislators must take care of the nation's laws. They do a great deal of that work in committees and subcommittees.

Working in Committees and Subcommittees

Our government has become so complicated that no one member of Congress can be an expert on all the issues that Congress must deal with. A committee system has evolved in Congress to divide up the work and allow members of Congress to develop expertise in various fields. Within both the Senate and the House of Representatives, there are committees and subcommittees whose members do research and write laws on all aspects of the nation's life. Senators and representatives are assigned to committees based on their expertise and party affiliation. They vote along party lines on issues. Committee members discuss and write bills and then send them to all of the members of the House or the Senate. Both the House and the Senate have committees on agriculture, appropriations, armed services, banking and the budget, foreign relations, the government, the judiciary, small businesses, and veterans' affairs.

In the early years of the country, the House and Senate

had very few committees, but as the country grew, the number of committees grew, too. The Senate now has sixteen committees that always exist, called standing committees. There are also many subcommittees that study certain aspects of the subjects considered by standing committees. The House has twenty-three standing committees, with even more subcommittees. The House and Senate committees can appoint and disband their subcommittees at will or when the work of the subcommittees is done. Committees are required to meet at least once a month. Committee and subcommittee members study a subject, sometimes for a year or more, before writing a bill for consideration.

Senate and House committees hold hearings on issues of importance concerning legislation before each body. Here, the Senate Judiciary Committee hears testimony from a witness during the hearing for Clarence Thomas's confirmation to the Supreme Court.

Another type of committee, called a select committee, exists only until its job is done. The House and Senate select intelligence committees are exceptions to the rule. They operate all the time and are in effect standing committees. The House and Senate have also created select and special committees to deal with special problems. There is really no difference between a select committee and a special committee except in the name.

In 1993 the Senate had two select committees, one on ethics and one on intelligence, and one special committee on aging. The House had one select committee on intelligence. The House used to have other select committees, including one on aging, and another on hunger, one on narcotics, and one on children, youth and families, but those select committees were disbanded in 1993 because the cost of maintaining them was too great. The purposes of those select committees were not abandoned, however. The standing committees of the House still bear responsibility for their problems. Select committees usually recommend legislation, but they don't consider bills. Standing committees are the ones that actually consider bills.

The House and Senate also have joint committees made up of both senators and representatives. These committees deal with problems such as printing. Each house has its own rules, but the Joint Committee on Printing works out the differences for printing projects that involve both the House and the Senate. A joint committee's membership reflects the percentage of Republicans and Democrats in the House and the Senate.

Conference committees are also made up of members of the House and Senate. Conference committees exist for only a short period of time—just long enough to settle differences between versions of bills that have been passed in the separate houses of Congress.

In the House of Representatives there is a group called the Committee of the Whole. This team can consider a bill without the 218-person majority of the 435 House members being present. Only 100 members of the House—known as the Committee of the Whole—need to be present to consider a bill. They recommend amendments and bills for the whole House to consider.

The route to the greatest power in Congress is through committee memberships and chairmanships in both the Senate and the House.

One of the oldest and most important standing committees in Congress is the House Rules Committee. It was set up in 1789, and it became a standing committee in 1880. Its members decide which legislation will get to the floor of the House. When other committees submit bills to the House, they're printed in the daily calendar. Then the House decides which bills are the highest-priority items. After that, the House Rules Committee prepares the agenda. That makes the House Rules Committee extremely important and influential.

Other important committees are the Armed Services Committee, the Senate Foreign Relations Committee, the House Foreign Affairs Committee, and the House and Senate Appropriations Committees, which have jurisdiction over federal spending.

Money to run the government comes from taxes. To get that money into the U.S. Treasury, the House Ways and Means Committee originates the tax laws and sends them to the Senate, which can amend them. After the laws are passed, the taxes raised are put into the Treasury. The House and Senate Budget Committees decide how much money will be spent in a given year, and then the House and Senate Appropriations Committees decide just how the money will be spent.

Members of Congress can achieve fame and power by serving as committee chairmen, and the legislators who head the committees that control the nation's purse strings are especially prominent people.

Chapter 4

Similarities and Differences between Representatives and Senators

The Senate and the House of Representatives share many duties and privileges. All members of Congress swear to uphold the Constitution of the nation when they take office. All members have the right to introduce legislation and to research and debate proposed legislation.

There are some important differences between senators and representatives, however, and to understand these differences, we must look at the history of Congress.

Terms and Election Procedures

As we already noted, some of the American patriots who created this republic wanted to have a powerful central government. Others thought that power should rest primarily in the hands of the thirteen separate states. So the founders decided to compromise. They chose not to put all the power in the hands of either the central government or the states. The founders gave the central government power over matters that concerned all Americans. The states kept the rest of the powers unless they were forbidden to do so by the Constitution. The founders made sure that the Senate and the House of Representatives would reflect this policy.

So, in those early days, two senators were elected by each state legislature—not by all of the people in a state voting in direct elections—for six-year terms. This arrangement allowed senators, who were elected for longer terms than representatives, to concentrate on the needs of the central government and to maintain a degree of freedom from the pressures of reelection. Also, as we have seen, only one-third of the Senate was elected at one time. The state legislatures continued to elect senators until Congress passed the Seventeenth Amendment to the Constitution in 1913. Ever since then, senators have been elected directly by the voters in statewide elections. Senators still serve six years in office, and elections are still staggered, so that the whole Senate is never replaced at one time.

The founders also decided that representatives should be elected directly by the people in their congressional districts—usually a portion of a city or a state. This way, the will of the people made itself known directly. As a result, the interests of individual voters have always been important to members of the House of Representatives. The House remained the only democratically elected institution in the federal government until the Seventeenth Amendment was passed.

Now that senators are also elected directly by all the people of a state, their responsibility to communicate with and to serve the voters is greater than it was before. But senators can still remain slightly removed from the hurly-burly of campaigning and focus their attention on executive concerns such as foreign affairs. The six-year term of office gives senators plenty of time to think.

The founders' provision that each state would have only two senators meant that small states would not be overwhelmed by the number and influence of senators from the more populous states. The heavily populated states do send more representatives to the House than the smaller states do. The more populous a state is, the more people are needed in Congress to represent the voters' views. By providing that the Senate has only two members from each state, and that the House has its membership based on the population of each state, the founders tried to make sure that there would be a balance of power within Congress. That's part of the system of checks and balances in the federal government.

Minority Members

Americans have become increasingly concerned about the small number of women and minority members in both houses of Congress. The House of Representatives has far more women and minority-group members than the Senate, but neither house of Congress precisely reflects the makeup of the general population. In the 103rd Congress, elected in

Newly elected senators (from left) Barbara Boxer, Dianne Feinstein, and Carol Moseley Braun pose with Senate Majority Leader George Mitchell in November 1992.

November 1992, for the first time in history, an African-American woman—Carol Moseley Braun, Democrat of Illinois—was elected to the Senate. She was only the second African American to win a Senate seat in the twentieth century. Senator Edward Brooke, Republican of Massachusetts, had been elected a few decades earlier, in 1967. The only other senators of African descent—four of them—were elected during the Reconstruction era following the Civil War in the nineteenth century. In 1994 there were six women senators in the 103d Congress. Five of them were Democrats.

The House of Representatives had thirty-nine African Americans and thirty-five women in 1994. But there are far more women and minority-group members in the popula- tion of the United States than the makeup of the House of Representatives suggests. Like the Senate, the House of Representatives is made up primarily of white males. One reason for this is that a person needs a great deal of money and influence to suc- cessfully campaign for elec- tion. Many successful candi- dates for Congress are lawyers. And the cost of education is so high that low- and middle-income people often cannot afford to attend college and law school. Without some type of advanced education, usually a law degree, a person cannot hope to find the money and influ- ence to mount an election campaign. It remains for future generations to find ways to change the composition of

Representative Kweisi Mfume from Maryland is the chair of the Congressional Black Caucus.

Congress so that it will reflect more accurately the ethnic groups, women, farmers, blue-collar workers, and other members of the general population of the country.

House Rules

The House and the Senate differ, too, in the way they conduct their business. One reason for this is that the House is so much larger than the Senate. The House of Representatives, with its 435 members, has to restrict the amount of time allowed for debate. Each House member is allowed to speak on the floor for a maximum of one hour. Unlimited debate in such a big legislative house could result in chaos.

The Senate, with only 100 members, has a different rule regarding debate. Any senator can speak for as long as he or she wants to about any piece of legislation before the full Senate. Every year senators consider changing that law, but so far they haven't done so, and they probably never will.

Some senators have spoken for several days at a time in order to delay the passage of a piece of legislation. Senators can talk about anything they want to. A southern senator once spoke for three days about all sorts of matters, including cooking and fishing techniques, in an attempt to hold up a vote on a piece of legislation he didn't like. This delaying tactic by a senator is called a filibuster.

The Senate can vote to stop debate. Sixteen senators must introduce the motion to end the filibuster. No action is allowed to be taken the second day, but on the third day the motion is put to a vote. Three-fifths of the Senate must vote for cloture—the closing off of debate.

There have been more filibusters in the Senate in the past two decades than in all the previous history of the country. One reason for this is that senators have become more independent-minded. Junior senators feel freer to speak their minds and to argue with senior Senate leaders. In the 1960s senators often delayed civil rights legislation by using the filibuster. This is a significant difference in the way the House and Senate conduct business.

In a famous scene from the motion picture Mr. Deeds Goes to Washington, *Jimmy Stewart filibusters to make his point heard.*

Chapter 5

The Leaders of the House and the Senate

The House Leaders

The Speaker of the House is by tradition a powerful, experienced representative from the majority party in the House. It takes many years for a member of Congress to become respected enough to reach that position. The Speaker is elected by other representatives—first by members of his own party, then by the full House. There's no reason why the Speaker cannot be a woman, but as yet no woman has been elected to that position.

The Speaker of the House has several important responsibilities. Along with the House Rules Committee, the Speaker decides which legislation gets to the floor of the House for consideration. The Speaker also has influence over committee assignments for members of his own party. He exercises his influence in a gathering of party members, called a caucus, where assignments are made. A majority whip, from the Speaker's own party, assists the Speaker with legislative tasks, such as recognizing members who wish to speak and state their positions on the floor of the House. The whip counts the votes. There are more Democrats than

Republicans in the 103rd Congress, and so the Speaker and the majority whip are both Democrats.

The House minority leader and the minority whip have the same jobs as the Speaker and his whip, but they are members of the minority party, so they develop the Republican position on issues.

The majority leader doesn't have to be a Democrat, but that is the way it has often worked out in the twentieth century. The last Republican Speaker of the House was Representative Joseph Martin of Massachusetts, in 1953 and 1954, under President Dwight D. Eisenhower.

The Senate Leaders

The U.S. vice president is the head of the Senate, but he exerts his influence as the Senate president only to break a tie vote. Either the president pro tempore of the Senate or the vice president can preside over the daily Senate sessions. However, they are usually busy with full schedules, so freshmen members of the majority party preside over most Senate sessions for one hour at a time. The vice president presides when a close vote or a tie is expected on an issue of particular importance.

By an informal arrangement, the real head of the Senate is the majority leader. That position, which developed during the twentieth century, is comparable to the Speaker's job in

President Bill Clinton gives his State of the Union address before a joint session of Congress. Behind him are Vice President Al Gore (left) and Speaker of the House Tom Foley (right).

the House. The Speaker of the House is mentioned in the U.S. Constitution, but the Senate majority leader is not. The Senate majority leader is elected by senators who belong to the political party with the most members in the Senate. Majority leaders have usually been Democrats in the twentieth century, though it's possible for Republicans to achieve a majority and elect the Senate majority leader. From 1980 to 1986, two Republican senators—Howard Baker and then Robert Dole—served as Senate majority leaders. A woman could serve as Senate majority leader, but so far none has ever done so.

The Senate majority leader is responsible for accomplishing the goals of the legislative programs. He also has great influence over the legislation considered by the Senate, because he can bring to the Senate floor the legislation that his party supports. In Democratic caucus meetings behind closed doors, he influences committee assignments for senators from his own party. And he serves as the principle source of information to members of his own party about the business of the Senate.

Senators who belong to the minority party in the Senate elect the minority leader. The Senate majority and minority leaders have assistants called whips, who are also senators. Whips help with legislative tasks such as getting legislation out of committees and onto the floor for consideration by all the senators.

Like all other members of Congress, the leaders of both houses have staff members who do secretarial and administrative work. These assistants are never legislators themselves.

Powerful Leaders in Congress

One of the most powerful congressional leaders in modern times was Lyndon Baines Johnson of Texas, who became President John F. Kennedy's vice president in 1960 and then entered the White House as president after Kennedy was assassinated in 1963. Johnson was famous for getting Congress to pass and fund legislation for domestic programs to benefit minority-group members, the poor, and the powerless. Most of the country's important civil rights laws were passed during his presidency, from 1963 to 1968. He was a

Newly elected congressman from Texas Lyndon Baines Johnson with his wife (left) and mother (right).

Senator Everett McKinley Dirksen from Illinois was a powerful orator and leader. A Senate office building is named in his honor.

masterful negotiator who had also spent many years as the Senate majority leader, and he had learned all about the personal lives and professional aims of his colleagues. He was able to twist their arms and persuade them to do what he wanted—or else he might expose matters they didn't want to be made public.

A powerful minority leader in the 1960s was Republican Senator Everett McKinley Dirksen of Illinois, a courtly, old-fashioned man who established a reputation as an orator with a golden voice and an ornate style. A political conservative, he once made a humorous comment about a call by Democrats for more spending: "A billion dollars here, a billion dollars there, and pretty soon you're talking about real money."

Dirksen was so highly regarded that a Senate office building was named for him. Speaker of the House Sam Rayburn, a Democrat from Texas, was similarly honored. A House office building bears his name. Rayburn, a bachelor who had no family responsibilities and who worked around the clock, was known to call members of the House in the middle of the night to discuss business. He devoted himself totally to his work. He helped promote the career of Lyndon Johnson when Johnson began his career in the federal government as a U.S. representative from Texas.

Chapter 6

Checks and Balances on the Lawmakers in Congress

The Supreme Court decides on the legality, or constitutionality, of all the country's laws. That right is provided for in the Constitution. So it's possible, in theory, for the Supreme Court to decide that a law passed by Congress is illegal. If a majority of the nine judges on the Supreme Court decrees that a law is unconstitutional, that law doesn't stay in effect, unless (1) Congress votes by a two-thirds majority to send the measure for a vote to the states, and then (2) three-fourths of the states ratify it by a constitutional amendment.

So the United States Congress, which makes the laws, runs under a system of checks and balances, just as the whole government does. This system strives to ensure that no one part of the government can become more powerful than another part. The system furthermore requires that all parts of the government cooperate and work together.

The founders wanted to make sure that the United States of America would never fall victim to the tyranny of one person, one special group, or one part of the government. That is why the founders provided for Congress to have certain special powers. For example, Congress has the right to approve or disapprove of treaties. It can also decide to accept or reject the people chosen by the president to serve on his cabinet—the secretary of state, for instance, and the attorney general. The president's nominees for judicial positions are also subject to the approval or disapproval of the Congress. (Some of the other powers of Congress are discussed in the next chapter.)

In short, Congress can't simply do whatever it wants to. The president and the Supreme Court and Congress watch each other's activities closely. Although the United States has some very powerful people in office, the country is run first and foremost by the laws upholding the Constitution and reflecting the will of the majority.

The system isn't perfect, of course. A Democratic president could have a lot of trouble getting a primarily Republican Congress to pass the laws that he thinks are best for the nation. A Republican president could face the same trouble with a Democratic Congress. In fact, a president could even have difficulties with a Congress dominated by members of his own party. For example, two Democratic presidents, Franklin D. Roosevelt and Harry S. Truman, faced strong opposition from largely Democratic legislatures that opposed their liberal legislative programs and ideas—programs that strove to involve the central government more in the affairs of individuals. So even without party politics coming into play, presidents and Congress don't always see eye to eye. When they disagree, both the president and the Congress must try to accomplish their goals through negotiations—"politicking"—behind the scenes. Each side usually gives up some goals and achieves others. The greatest legislators have always been forceful negotiators who have a deep understanding of the legislative process, and who have the best interests of the people of the United States at heart.

"politicking"

Chapter 7

Special Powers of the Congress

Congress has other mighty responsibilities aside from the making of laws. The Senate and the House of Representatives are also responsible for maintaining the country's armed forces, assessing taxes, borrowing money, printing money, and regulating commerce. As part of the system of checks and balances, the Senate has the task of advising and consenting to treaties with other countries about all sorts of matters, such as agreements to end wars or to regulate trade. The Senate also has the power to approve or disapprove nominations by the president—for example, the nominations of Supreme Court justices. That power of the Senate is also part of the system of checks and balances. The House of Representatives is responsible for presenting impeachment charges when an official is removed from office. In an impeachment proceeding, the House functions as a grand jury, investigating the charges, while the Senate acts as a court to try the impeachment case.

Both Houses meet in a joint session of Congress on January 6—after a presidential election—to count the electoral votes. Each state is assigned a certain number of elec-

The power to impeach judges and the president is given to the House of Representatives. Above is a roll call tally of the vote taken in 1974 to impeach President Richard M. Nixon. Senate committees must approve presidential nominations to certain offices. (Right) Anita Hill being sworn in before the Senate Judiciary Committee hearing testimony on Clarence Thomas's nomination to the Supreme Court.

toral votes based on the population of the state. If no candidate receives a majority of the total electoral votes, the House of Representatives chooses the president from among the three candidates having the largest number of votes, and the Senate chooses the vice president from the two candidates having the largest number of votes for that office.

It is hard to imagine now that when Congress was first set up, neither senators nor representatives thought of govern-

Senators look on as electoral votes are counted in the Senate in 1993. The election of the president is not official until this process is completed.

ment service as a full-time career. The original House of Representatives had only sixty-five members, and the first Senate had only twenty-six. The legislators worked at their usual jobs in their home states for about eleven months of the year and spent only about a month in Washington, D.C. Today legislators must sometimes work from early morning until late at night, year round, to get the country's business done. This gives you some idea of how much larger and more complicated the central government of the United States has become. Congress now passes laws to govern a world superpower.

All the while, Congress must strive to maintain its integrity. From time to time, legislators have found it necessary to investigate their own activities—sometimes the activities of

From time to time, senators and congressmen betray the trust of their constituents. (Left) Dan Rostenkowski was indicted in 1994 on a number of criminal charges. (Below) Members from the National Organization of Women protest against Senator Bob Packwood, who had been accused by many women of sexual harassment.

groups within Congress that have been accused of abusing their powers, sometimes charges of the misuse of power or influence by a single member of the Senate or the House. Members of Congress have been reprimanded, censured, and even expelled by their own colleagues. Others have had their questionable activities exposed and publicized to the degree that the voters back home have refused to reelect them. Or legislators may simply be pressured to resign. The many ways that Congress regulates the conduct of its members is based on a constitutional provision stating that congressmen may punish members for disorderly behavior and, with two-thirds of either house, may expel a member.

No matter how painful the task has been at times, members of Congress, sometimes crossing party lines, know that they must ensure that the government operates under laws to protect American citizens from any kind of tyranny abroad or within the United States, and to maintain the integrity and strength of Congress so that it functions as a partner in government and is never subservient to any other part of the government. As one of the three branches of the federal government, Congress must perpetuate and enhance, and never dilute, the democratic spirit of the U.S. Constitution.

For Further Reading

Ragsdale, Bruce A. *The House of Representatives.* New York: Chelsea House, 1989.

Richie, Donald A. *The Senate.* New York: Chelsea House, 1988.

————. *The Young Oxford Companion to the Congress of the United States.* New York: Oxford University Press, 1993.

Stern, Gary M. *The Congress: America's Lawmakers.* Austin, Tex.: Raintree Steck-Vaughn, 1992.

Index

About the Author

Leslie Gourse has done research and written stories for major news organizations, particularly CBS Network Radio News and the national desk of *The New York Times*. She worked for CBS from 1966 to 1968 and for the *Times* from 1968 to 1974, spending her last four years at the paper on assignment for the national desk. Among other pieces, she wrote stories about the federal government, especially during the congressional investigations of President Richard M. Nixon and the Watergate scandal.

Since 1974, Ms. Gourse has been a freelance writer for many major magazines and newspapers covering general culture, social trends, and music. Her most recent books have been about current and historic New York City, jazz musicians, and jazz history. She lives in New York City.